An Unquiet Life

Poems from the Edge of Ache and Awe

Neha Jhingon

Copyright © Neha Jhingon
All Rights Reserved.

This book has been self-published with all reasonable efforts taken to make the material error-free by the author. No part of this book shall be used, reproduced in any manner whatsoever without written permission from the author, except in the case of brief quotations embodied in critical articles and reviews.

The Author of this book is solely responsible and liable for its content including but not limited to the views, representations, descriptions, statements, information, opinions, and references ["Content"]. The Content of this book shall not constitute or be construed or deemed to reflect the opinion or expression of the Publisher or Editor. Neither the Publisher nor Editor endorse or approve the Content of this book or guarantee the reliability, accuracy, or completeness of the Content published herein and do not make any representations or warranties of any kind, express or implied, including but not limited to the implied warranties of merchantability, fitness for a particular purpose.

The Publisher and Editor shall not be liable whatsoever...

Made with ♥ on the BookLeaf Publishing Platform
www.bookleafpub.in
www.bookleafpub.com

Dedication

To my family and friends—
Thank you for holding me through every storm and season. Your steady love, your laughter, your belief in me —these are the quiet miracles that carried me home.

To my daughter, Saanvi—
You are my anchor in this world. Your laughter is my light, your presence my peace. You remind me daily of joy's quiet power, of love's true form. You are, and will always be, the most radiant poem I've ever been gifted to witness.

To life—
Thank you for the ache, the awe, the fire, and the fall. Thank you for giving me not just experience, but the *eyes to notice*, the *heart to hold*, and the *pen to shape* it into something I could survive—and maybe even offer.

This book is for all the selves I've been, and for the ones still waiting to speak.
Thank you for allowing me to live—**an unquiet life.**

Preface

This is not the story of a life lived quietly.

An Unquiet Life is a collection of poems written in the margins of days—between the first breath of morning and the last sigh of night, between the roles I've played and the woman I've slowly uncovered underneath them all. These poems were born not in resolution, but in restlessness. They emerged from love and rupture, from silence and song, from the aching gaps between what was lived and what was never said. In writing them, I was not seeking to define my life, but to *witness it*—with honesty, with curiosity, and with as much grace as I could muster.

The poems are arranged into seven sections, each reflecting a distinct phase or emotional landscape. While life is rarely linear, there is a natural progression in these pages—from questioning and formation, through love and grief, to eventual arrival at a quieter kind of clarity.

The first section, **Echoes of Womanhood**, speaks to my earliest reckonings—with what it meant to be a woman, with what was passed down to me, and with the stories I was expected to carry. These poems explore inherited silences and myths, the invisible weight of expectations, and the moments of rebellion that cracked them open. The feminine in this section is both sacred and ordinary —at times mythic and ancestral, at others confused, yearning, burning, or quietly becoming.

In **Love and Its Undercurrents**, I dive into the elemental force of connection—its tenderness, its disillusionments, its hunger and hauntings. Love here is not a tidy resolution. It comes uninvited, lingers in unexpected places, leaves traces like breadcrumbs or burns like solar flares. Some poems whisper of touch and longing; others rage or retreat. Together, they chart the tidal nature of intimacy—how it carries us, crashes over us, and sometimes remakes us entirely.

The third section, **Wounds and Endings**, is perhaps the most vulnerable. It holds the sharp edges of separation, of pain that lingers long after goodbye, of grief that arrives and refuses to leave. These poems do not offer closure so much as witness. They sit with heartbreak. They name what was lost. They honour the truth that even endings deserve to be seen.

The Mess and the Madness brings a tonal shift—a leaning into the absurdities and complications of daily life. There is humour here, but also quiet truth. These poems speak to the chaos of the ordinary: the broken shower, the out-of-control morning, the ragged rituals of living. They allow space for contradiction—for wanting, for wondering, for collapsing in the middle of a Tuesday and still getting up again.

In **Inherited Fires**, I turn inward—toward memory, legacy, and the subterranean layers of family. These poems honour the women I come from and the child I raise. They ask what we carry forward, and what we choose to set down. They reflect on the tension between resilience and softness, tradition and choice, mothering and selfhood. This section is quieter, more reflective, a kind of reckoning with origin.

Of Goodbyes and Grace and Gratitude is a soft place to land. It is a letting-go space. Here, I explore farewells that don't always have neat endings—griefs without graves, relationships that dissolve without closure, and the unexpected moments of grace that still manage to bloom in the wake of loss. These poems are elegiac but hopeful. They are the hush after the storm.

Finally, **The Land of Belonging** offers a return—to breath, to body, to something like peace. It is not a triumphal arrival, but a gentle homecoming. In these poems, there is awe again. There is softness. There is the slow rebuilding of trust in one's own skin. This section whispers more than it declares, but it stands as the quiet exhale at the end of a long, unquiet song.

This collection, in its entirety, is my offering. It is the record of a life that does not sit still, that questions, aches, longs, laughs, remembers, and continues. If somewhere within these pages you find yourself—your voice, your shadow, your breath—I hope you feel seen.

With tenderness,

Neha

Acknowledgements

This book began as a quiet whisper, a hesitant reaching into the dark, and it would never have taken form without the light and love of those who stood beside me as I slowly gave voice to my unquiet heart.

To my family—thank you for your patience, your warmth, and the strength you've given me through every season of becoming. You've allowed me the space to feel, to falter, to rise again, and for that, I am forever grateful.
To my dearest friends, who have read drafts, listened to rambled ideas, and held space when the words refused to come—you are the constellation I've looked to when I lost my way. Thank you for never letting me forget that I am seen, heard, and deeply loved.

To my daughter, Saanvi—your laughter, your brilliance, and your boundless spirit are woven into every page of this collection. You are the truest poem I know. Thank you for anchoring me in joy and reminding me why beauty and truth are worth writing toward.

To the artists, poets, and women whose voices have shaped my inner landscape—some living, some ancestral

—I owe you more than words. Your work gave me permission to speak in my own language, to feel without shame, and to trust the rhythm of my own pulse.

To the solitude, the stillness, the sorrow, and the sacred mess of life—thank you. You gave me material, yes—but more importantly, you gave me meaning.
Finally, to every reader who finds resonance here: thank you for stepping into this space with me. Poetry only becomes real when it meets another breath. I hope these pages offer you companionship, courage, or comfort— however fleeting, however fierce.

Part 1. Echoes of Womanhood

In a world that moulds women with rituals and roles, these poems resist quiet conformity. Here, womanhood is not a fixed silhouette—it is iridescent, fierce, soft, spiritual, inherited, and reclaimed. I have written this section to give voice to the multiplicity of being female in a world that constantly seeks to define me.

1. The One Who Lights Lamps

Have you heard the tinkle of her laughter?
It floats like wisps of light—
bursting through a mottled sky,
wildfires blooming in her chest.

She plants them in a garden bed
of muddled sunshine,
that kisses the feet of the one she loves.

And beyond the bower, where wildflowers sleep,
lies the temple of her desires—
where each night, she lights a flame.

Have you seen her glowing feet?
Planted firm upon the earth—
but her hair?
Ah, her hair holds tales:
fire-breathing tresses, unruly,
untamed by the bravest wranglers.

She is the tempest.

A single tear could stir the oceans.

She, the one adorned in flame,
who worships the shadow of her lover
and laughs in songs.

2. Love, Creation and Life

The calm azures, sunning themselves
beneath the noonday sky,
never saw the trickle
of inky blues—drip by drip.
The setting sun smiled slyly
at the conflation:

Enjoy the dance of hues—
resisting and accepting,
Attai meeting Abbasi—
swallowing him whole,
playfully, yet resolutely.

The universe watched with bated breath,
awaiting the cosmic humdrum
that would surely spew stars,
planets,
a thudding pulse of new rhythm.

Handprints—

the secret language spoken
only between the two.

Sighs, louder than thunder,
plunging the weary into wakefulness.

And when the violent coupling
reached its inevitable climax—

Anansa gushed through lands
poisoned by war,
inviting life
to feed on her supple breast.

Now, no one can say
where the azure was—
or where the ink went.

3. Am I a Woman?

There are many ways to be a woman—
our goddesses have chosen their own form.
And yet he scorns the way I choose
to live in freedom, unconfined—
my will unchained from him, in flesh or vow.

"Where is your vermilion?" he demands,
as if I should be crushed
beneath the weight of his accusation.

"You do not wear the black-bead chain
that tells the world you belong to me."
Did I? Did I belong to him—
like Shakti bound to Shiva's flame?
Or did he seek that obedient girl
his mother dreamed into being—
the one who bends, who waits, who yields?

Because I crown my hair with fire,
I became less of a woman to him.

But there are many ways to be a woman.
Our goddesses have chosen their own form—
and so I choose mine.

The one who shines in iridescent light,
who fears no man, no silence, no night.
The one who walks alone, unled,
planting gardens of joy where her footsteps tread,
belonging to no one but herself.

4. Ochre is My Colour

Red—why is the colour of love always red?
Like the sweltering sting of an open gash.
Why not ochre—
like the flame's quiet tip
that curls around a pile of logs,
an all-consuming rhapsody of truth?

I like ochre—limonite calls me,
pulling me into a prehistoric odyssey,
as ancient, perhaps, as love itself.
Ochre—born of iron's oxide breath—
persistent, stable, defiant of time.
Why not that, then?

Ochre—fields of mineral earth,
just waiting to be scoured
for pigment rich enough to cling to my brush,
even after its torrid affair
with cold-pressed sheets has ended.

Still, I understand red.
Why not?
For many hearts have broken in love,
and left behind only the red—
of the wound that would not close.

5. This Body

This body has witnessed much—
love and hate, trepidation,
the weight of expectation,
the lift of elation.

It has tasted the acid of anxiety,
the gushing flow of sobriety.
It has swallowed heat, radiated warmth,
glowed in a lover's arms,
and shattered on solitary days.

It has glowered with rage,
melted with gratitude.
It has been home to many,
and homage to even more.

It has stretched for the miracle of life,
and bent for the spirit to grow.
It has broken in a fit of fury,
then pieced itself back

in the shape of strength.

It has yearned—and been yearned for.
It has burned—and been burned for.

This body: a temple, a time machine.
This body: a vessel, a record keeper.
This body: stretched taut across memory.
This body: curled tight, ready to be tossed.

This body.
This body.

6. Sacred Things

This heart—
forged of glass and fairy dust—
a delicate balance of pleasure and pain,
holds memories both distant and near:
echoes of laughter, whispers of tears.
Each fragment a story, each crack a truth,
worn by time—yet standing firm.

It belongs not in harems of fleeting desire,
but in a sacred temple bathed in light,
where love pours forth like the Amazon's rush—
a current of warmth through wild expanse,
a world of wonder, of miracles spun,
tugging gently at the red thread of fate.

So tread with care upon this hallowed ground—
you are in the presence of the thing that matters:
the pulse of a universe, the breath of a dream,
each beat a season, each throb a tide,
a dance of shadows and sunlit grace,

a symphony of souls, forever entwined.

Here, the air is thick with promise and pain,
a tapestry stitched with hope's golden threads,
where despair's shadow still softly lingers.
Yet, within the chaos, a candle glows—
guiding the way through darkened valleys,
reminding us: love is both tempest and balm.

So come—come with reverence, come with intent.
Unwrap your heart like a sacred gift.
Offer your essence—your fears, your joys—
and in return, receive the infinite:
a bond unbreakable, forged in fire,
of every moment that brought us here. Together.

7. An Ode to Myself

Some days, my head is a darkened cloud,
drifting in slow, sluggish flight
across the blue canvas of possibility.
But no matter how heavy it grows,
there's always a silver thread—
it flies, still, with a glowing light.

Some days, my body is a cornucopia—
ripe and bursting with joy and grief,
spilling itself with reckless grace.
To be one with the clouds, it must give—
and give it does, with childlike glee,
a tickle that laughs from skin to sky.

Some days, my thoughts are oranges—
peeled and perfumed, citrusy bright,
offered to strangers in quiet delight.
They chuckle softly, surprised by the sour;
and on other days, beneath the peel,
nectarines shimmer in plain sight.

Some days, I am a force of nature.
Other days, a cloud adrift,
with only the promise of rain to give.
Some days, a vessel of words and hush;
on others, a fever—pure, electric.

But always, always—
remember:
I am a vendor of delights.

Part 2. Love and Its Undercurrents

Desire does not arrive quietly. It seeps in through glances and silences, floods the body like song. These poems navigate eros, connection, and the ineffable pull between two souls—sometimes divine, sometimes derailed, always intense. Love here is cosmic, disorienting, tender, and wild.

8. Lovemaking

Stark crazy. Raving mad. Or is it not?
You don't know—only that it feels good.
Free-falling. You write of it endlessly.
Abysses—your favorites, always.

Effort, immense. One-word replies.
Single-nodded conversations.
Free-falling. Again.

Luring smiles. Warm sighs,
Cool wind on your face.
Smuggled stances. Glazed glances.

Clockwork—stopped.
Moments—faltering.
Fingers on lips.
Hands on shoulders.

Pulling you in.
Letting go.

Whispering winds.
Bellowing silences.

Reverberating moans.
Psychedelic rhapsodies.
Resonating heaves.

Is it war?
Or is it endless lovemaking
with the vibrations of the cosmos?

9. Drunk as Drunk Could Be

Drunk on the possibilities of what could be,
I waver—stagger in and out of your threshold,
just as you do mine.

Surreptitious, like the ocean's spray
lingering on the jagged cliffs—
your hands hover around mine,
long enough for me to feel
the throb of your pulse
pressing against my wrist.

We are alive, you and I—
and we are counting sunsets.

While you hum your songs
beneath the moonlit night,
I am thinking of that crescent moon
you once pointed out to me—
and wondering if you're wondering
about me, too.

10. Off to sea

The clock chimes six—
and still the day refuses
to melt into night.

I watch the orange sun
slowly dissolve
into pink clouds,
but nightfall
remains just out of reach.

I look again—
only one hour has passed
since my eyes met the clock's face.

Seven.

But it is nine—
the hour you will finally
cross this threshold.

And between now and then,
an eternity still waits—
before I can be drunk on you.

I want to drift off to sea,
hailing the horizons
where time holds no meaning—
where these wretched hours
that pry you from me
can never wedge themselves
between our breath.

Let the sky's hot rim
burn as feverish
as your flesh and mine.

Let our lips
never again taste
the bitterness
of land.

11. Love Song for the Living

Every parting from you
feels like a long, endless sigh—
like all is escaping
into the gaping void
my world becomes
when you are not in it.

This life is a cauterized wound—
and it puckers in your absence,
like a dried peach pit.

So next you come, my love,
stay—
and rain on me.

And I promise
to cradle you
in flower boughs
and such.

12. Desire

There is this delicate desire
In my heart,
to pulse through Your veins,
like you do through mine

13. Embrace

At the corner of your lips,
I've watched moments falter—
each time that upward curve
creases the lines on your face.

It's not that I haven't seen
time pause before.
I have—been privy
to that strange, cruel trick of nature.

But still, I wonder:
why is it only your feet
can stop the turning of tides,
and only your scent
can quiet the world?

14. If Wishes Had Wings

What if you stayed tonight—
and we didn't go to bed?
What if we dipped our toes
into the warm creek's edge,
and laughed like children
until the sun came up?

What if we danced with fireflies,
and followed them into the woods?
What if we found their hidden place,
lay down upon the forest floor—
and kissed, this time,
while time just passed us by?

15. Vocabulary of Longing (A Poem in Two Parts)

She

My eyes scan the room for you—
I haven't even taken off
my coat, my scarf,
or braced for the hostess's glare.

But already, I'm searching—
my gaze aching to land on you.

And then—Eureka!
Corduroy legs, slouched deep in the only chair
big enough to cradle your wildness.

Long curls cascade, untamed.
Your beard—flecked silver in the dim light—
glistens like a secret.

Then you look at me.

Our eyes lock—
and I melt.
A puddle on the hardwood floor.

Caution: Wet!
Did the hostess notice me blush?

I feel you staring—
did the music stop?
Is everyone watching us?
Or just my imagination, again?

Did you just undress me with your eyes?
Did your lips move, softly,
whispering my name—
or is it just my mind
playing tricks on me?

He

Damn. You're not here yet.
I've scanned every face,
but none of them are yours.

I didn't even want to come—
but one glimpse of you
would've made it worth it.

Where are you?
I'll take the big chair,
just in case
you feel like sharing.

I have to stay sharp—
you could walk in any second.

Wait—
is that you by the door?
Pin-straight hair streaked
with green and blue?
Who else could it be?

Damn, you light up the room.
This place doesn't deserve that smile.

Are you unbuttoning your coat now?
God, let me help you—
or at least imagine
my fingers tracing your skin.

And now you're looking at me.

Shit.
You caught me mid-fantasy.

I was thinking
how much I want to pull you
out of this noisy crowd.

Would you forgive me
for wanting that?

Wait—
did I just see you blush?

Sweetheart,
read my lips—
come to me now.

I'm calling you,
my siren.

16. The Red Thread of Fate

There is this longing in me—
lyrical at times,
foreboding at others—
but always ripe,
brimming with patience and desire.

It is like a pomegranate,
its fleshy pearls
wetting your fingers,
leaving a red trail
along your chin,
staining your clothes,
ruining the carpet.

My longing—pearl-like—
strung along a silken thread
that binds me to you.

My longing:
the red thread of fate—

running through lifetimes,
crossing continents and dimensions.

Tell me—
do you feel its tug, too?

17. Getting Lost With You

It bodes well for me
that you love long-winded stories—
the kind where I set off from college
and wind into my childhood,
then pause to check
if the dog's bowl is empty.

I'd tell you how grateful I am
for your ear—
how you listen to my ramblings—
but you know that already.

Why else would you hold my hand,
or my waist,
when you're feeling frisky,
meandering with me
through the maze of my thoughts,
always bringing me home before dinner?

Still, I thank you, my love,

for the stories you take from me—
and the ones you leave behind—
for always getting lost with me
on roads we never travel twice.

18. An Ode to Him

I knew you, right when my gaze first fell upon you,
sculpted in the dawn's first light, you rise like the
mountains—
each ridge and valley, etched with the hand of time.
Your arms, twin branches of an ancient oak,
stretch wide to gather the world, to cradle the sun,
to carry the weight of the heavens with a silent, steadfast
grace.

Your chest, the broad expanse of the sea,
tells the stories of storms, of tides that have risen and
fallen, of battles won in the silence of night,
where the moon rests her face
against the soft, warm curve of your breath.
Hands, calloused and strong,
that have tilled the stubborn earth, that have held love
like a fragile bird.

Your fingers are the roots of trees,
anchoring the earth to the pulse of your heart.

Your back, a canvas of muscle and sinew,
a map of journeys taken and roads left to wander,
the language of sweat and soil, firm and unyielding,
you stride through my heart, leaving footprints like
whispers
that will linger long after, the world has turned to dusk.

19. Longing

In the river of consciousness
I dropped a tear of longing
And now the whole world is lit up
With a desire for you

20. Aftermath

That stray hair on my pillow
That does not belong to my head
Is an intruder, a tattle-tale
A reminder of the games that we play
And the aftermath of love.

Part 3. Wounds and Endings

What follows love is often more revealing than love itself. This section is an archaeology of heartbreak, betrayal, and the quiet strength of closure. These poems speak of doors left ajar too long, of crossroads not taken together, and of the grace that follows grief.

21. Closing the Door

I'd like to think you were a mistake—
someone who slipped through an open door,
left ajar not by intent,
but by carelessness.

But that would be a lie.
This door—
the one meant to guard me
from foes, from rot,
from the ugly things
that litter this world—
has never been closed.

Not once.
Not in this lifetime.

So can I blame the door
for letting you in?
Not really. I cannot.

You came and went as you pleased,
and I let you.
The door was always open.

But now, the stars are fading,
and dawn is breaking.
I am ready to meet this day.

And the first thing I will do—
is close the door.

So that you,
who left of your own accord,
can no longer
walk back in.

22. The Crossroads

And when the crossroads came,
you chased the bright light—
convinced it marked the end of your tunnel.

I stayed a while, nursing my pain,
imagining your hand still in mine—
but we never spoke the same language.

My love, you spoke with your hands;
I, with my tears—
the ones that soaked my pillow every night.

But the crossroads are no longer
where you'll find me, alone and pining.
I stand tall now, like the redwoods—

I rise above the clouds,
for I was always rooted deeper than you.
Love helped me grow
in ways I never imagined.

I am red and yellow—
all the colors of the rainbow.
I am the seven notes strung into a rhapsody.
We were never the same—
and now, even less so.

We never truly spoke the same language—
you, with your anger;
me, with my eyes.

So the crossroads are no longer
where you'll find me—
head in hands, waiting.

I am flowing now, like the summer wind,
carrying the seeds of the redwood—

in search of the fire
that will breathe them alive;
in search of the hands and heart
that won't flinch at warmth;

in search of the light
that's not the end of any tunnel—
but the beginning of home.

23. The Beginning of the End

And in the end,
it was the distance
between my turned back
and yours,
that was impossible
to traverse.

24. Regrets

Have you ever felt the urge
to stare into a star-stung night,
and invite the past
to look into you?

You rest your head on green, soft grass,
thinking of the boy
who once asked you
to pass through his burnt hands—
the one whose gods
you danced with,
pitch-drunk on love.

Sure, you can sift through
the memory-dust of wordsmiths,
philanderers,
and the one who got away—
the one buying Birkin bags
for his white wife.

But can you let the past
really look into you?
Into the eyes of the eight-year-old
who once locked herself
in a coat rack—
decades ago—
wondering how far along
the sweet release of eternity lay?

Or the girl
who searched for happy endings
in pages full of magic and ruin?

Yes, you can let the past look in.
At your seersucker life—
striped in red and blue.
And if offered it again,
you'd still swallow that red pill.

Only this time—
you'd pass through that silly boy's hands,
and burn them yourself.

25. The Sunflowers

When you come to meet me,
bring that yellow sunflower—
the one you plucked
from the hillside
where wild things run free.

Fill your pockets with sunlight—
the kind that filters through the tree
grown from those apple seeds
you tossed without care,
once upon a time.

And I'll bring my best self—
just how you like it:
silent and smiling,
pretending not to bleed.

So that when you stab me with your fork,
reminiscing carelessly
about the girl

you kissed all night last year,

we can both laugh—

and watch the sunflower
turn toward the fading sun.

26. The Crumbs in My Bed

You joke about throwing me a bone—
and I wonder if you chuckled to yourself
last night,
while leaving breadcrumbs down the hallway,
before you ended up in my bed.

I am not a lost child
in need of saving.
I'm not a tourist
with a checkout date.

So why the bone?

To please the animal in me—
the one not satisfied with crumbs?
Or to place the weight of gravity
on the needle's edge—
all flesh and bone and balance?

What comes next? I wonder,

steeping my morning tea
in a sea of regret,
nursing a small hurricane
rising in my chest.

27. Reclamation

I will recede slowly from your life—
bit by bit,
again and again—
like the wave
that just kissed the shore
and slipped away.

And just as the wet sand
stands as the only witness
to that mercurial touch—

the taste of my name
on your tongue
will be the final trace
of my fleeting presence
in your arms.

Part 4. The Mess and the Madness

Some days unravel slowly; others implode with fury.
Here are the poems of ordinary chaos, mental spirals,
and the elastic tension between trying to hold it all
together and letting it all fall apart. These are testaments
to survival in the smallest of daily moments.

28. Loneliness

Loneliness is a frequent visitor—
a familiar twinge
in this tattered heart.

On Sundays,
it seeps into my home
and seats itself at the brunch table,
glaring smugly at me from across.

And as I sink my teeth
into fleshy mangoes—
ripened by the May sun—
it reminds me
of a childhood
fraught with the heaviness
of other people's fear and anger—
their loneliness.

Loneliness—
she is a familiar guest.

Nay, an intimate one.

She has shared my bed,
spanning the distance
between my turned back
and his—
on cold nights,
and warm ones.

She has touched me—
most invasively—
on crowded streets,
amidst loud cheers,
in hugs,
and perhaps
even a kiss or two.

Loneliness has morphed
into many shapes,
fit into many silhouettes,
and seamlessly clung
to the skin between my fingers.

I wear her proudly,
like a second skin—
forgetting, sometimes,

where I end
and she begins.

54

29. Dirge

Has it ever happened to you—
that words you'd long forgotten—
nouns, verbs, adjectives—
suddenly surface
from the depths of a mind
you've no stomach to fathom?

You could shine a light under there,
try to see where
these buried syllables emerge from—
but you hesitate.

Afraid, perhaps,
of what lies beneath the layers of time.

Then—
a word swims up,
just as you're pondering
the weight of this excavation:

Cabron.

It stings the mouth—
a bitter splash of acid and mirth.

Cabron.

A word that was never yours,
never part of your tongue—
but somehow,
it signals the end.

A two-syllabled dirge
that silences the fear
that once devoured you.

Tomorrow—
we shine a light.
We clean house.

30. An Ode to This Messy Life

And then there are others—
with perfect teeth,
beautiful hair,
shoelaces tied tight,
homes spotless,
hearts light and skipping.

And then—there's me.

This ragged row of teeth,
punished just for being mine.
This dull nest of hay
I wear proud upon my head.

Shoelaces dangling—
afraid to stretch too far.
My house, a mess of spaces
that do not want me—
that have come to abhor me.

My heart, rancid with past hurts—
still festering, still oozing.

But for all their polish,
what do they know of life?

I sailed high seas,
tasted the salt of disappointment
as it cracked my lips
and drew blood.

I climbed summits—
then tripped on angry laces,
tumbled down
into piles of steaming trash.

My body wears scars—
gifts from love too deep
and love gone wrong.

So now, when I walk among them,
you can spot me from afar—

this crooked smile, my badge of honor;
this clump of greying hair,
my certificate from the trenches.

These wild, worn shoelaces—
testimony of every summit lost.

My messy house—proof
that I've been everywhere
and arrived nowhere.

And this heart—putrid with over-loving,
aching too much,
breaking too often.

Still, when life calls,
I show up.

Again and again.

Ready to be broken,
to slip from heights,
to stand,
soaked to the bone
in unrelenting rain.

31. Out of Control

This morning, when I woke up,
I had no idea my day would fall apart.

The water won't stay hot enough—
it runs from lukewarm to cold
in minutes.
I'm shivering beneath it,
wondering where all the warmth went.

The shampoo won't budge
from the bottle's stubborn bottom.
It clings for dear life,
afraid of the mess
my hair has become.

The dress I laid out last night
won't fit today.
I swear it's in a pact
with the dryer—
pulling a cruel little prank.

And don't get me started
on the car.
No really—don't.
Because it just won't start.

And as if the day needed
one more twist—
there you are,
running late again
for the thousandth time.

So when I woke up this morning,
I was braced for irony and heartbreak—
but this day?
This silly, spiraling day
just went completely
out of control.

Somewhere,
someone named Murphy
is rolling on the floor,
laughing in a sea of
I told you so's.

32. The Voices

The angry voices in my head
get very loud—some days,
they pluck moments from my past
and hurl them at my face.

They will me to hurt—
to bleed from the sharp corners
meant to cut like knives.

And yet,
I keep smiling—
trying to calm these voices
the way only a mother
soothes a petulant child.

33. Fifty Shades of Chaos

Just as the dark settles
into the numbness of night,
she unleashes fifty shades of chaos.

She lets them pirouette
across the shadows of silent dreams
that loom behind wide-open eyes.

She's mastered the art of war—
on herself.
And the demons
that won't let her sleep
will one day lie bleeding in the gutter,
wounds hidden
where no light dares to fall.

So she sits, silently,
warming her hands
by the raging fires of her spirit.

And in this madness,
there is no turning back.

It is fifty shades of chaos—
and it is all happening
here.

34. Insomnia

I've been clinging to a poem
that refuses to let go.

It's lodged somewhere in my throat—
tickling, choking—
haunting my dreams.

It flickers against closed eyes,
like a candle flaring,
angry in the wind.

It lulls me
into a false sense of control.
But on lonely nights,
it snickers behind clenched teeth,
reminding me
of the vastness of my empty bed—
taunting me,
reminding me who's in charge.

I've tried to cough it out,
weary from this sleepless haunting.

And still, it clings—
this poem.

Like monsoon clouds
eclipsing a full moon,
leaving nothing
but a ghost
for the world to see.

Part 5. Inherited Fires

We carry stories not just in our memories, but in our
bodies. Passed from womb to womb, these legacies often
arrive uninvited—fire, silence, sacrifice, and resilience.
These poems trace the gifts and ghosts we inherit, and
the transformations we attempt.

35. A Gift For My Daughter

The fires of my mother's womb
forged this tiny body—
and pushed me forth, crying,
into a strange world
that has cradled me
in both roses and thorns.

She is a sharer of gifts, my mother.
She adorned me
with her mother's patience,
gifted me
her grandmother's resilience.
My timidity—
I received from her too.

And so,
I inherited the fires of my womb—
flames that burn within,
consume me at times.

But for my daughter,
I wish to withhold these gifts.

To her,
I will not pass down patience.
Nor resilience.

Instead,
I give her my fire,
my rebellion,
my light-footed joy.

To her,
I give the woman
I have forged in me.

36. Things We Carry

I emptied my pockets today—
found a black clip, bent backward—
something my daughter thrust into my hand
before climbing the monkey bars.

There was some lint,
a thread unraveled
from the pocket of these old denims
that cling to my hips
like second skin—
tight, unforgiving,
hard to peel off
since I gained the weight.

Among the things I carry:
my child's carelessness,
dust from things
that once mattered—
and this realization—
that my body has grown heavier

from guilt and lamentation
I never set down.

But today,
I am emptying my pockets—
turning them inside out,
and shedding all
that no longer belongs to me.

37. Lessons in Forgetting

For every flower
you picked from my garden,
I lit a thousand lamps.

But now—
the garden is barren,
and my house
has burned to the ground.

38. The Arms That Once Held Me

Those arms—
their hollows scented
with sweet molasses
and saline sweat—
were once my haven,
my home.

Now, they're gone—
no longer there
to hold me.

But I'd recognize them
anywhere in the world,
by their smell alone—
the scent that reminds me
of home.

Part 6. Goodbyes, Grace and Gratitude

There are losses that never announce themselves and storms that arrive inside the soul. These poems are elegies—for relationships, for innocence, for the self we once were. They hold space for pain, and for the quiet rituals of parting and remembrance.

39. Of Goodbyes and Tears

Will you stay
and build me a boat?

The storm inside me
is rising—
raging me to the edge.

And if you can't
hold my hand long enough,
then help me build that boat—

so I can weather the storm
that will follow
your footsteps
out my door.

40. Wounds

The changing silhouette
of your smile
tells me—
just how the world
has salted your wounds.

41. Heartache

As tongues of fire
lovingly wrap themselves
around the last log of pine—

so do your arms
sear through this skin—
the sheath that holds
my heart
and all it guards
from spilling out.

42. Forgotten

Layers of dust mean
Not that all is forgotten
Only that the dust is settled

43. The Big Bad World

They've told me
what a dark place this world is.

Still, I traverse its length and breadth
with wide-eyed wonder.

There are monsters—
not just in closets—
but loose on the streets,
roaming freely.

A well-wisher once warned me.
And like always,
I nodded—
used to well-meaning words
that remain just that:
words.

I know—
when the monsters come for me,

I'll face them alone.
Unarmed.

And yet,
it's hard to persuade me
to squint at the world
through the prism of fear,
or past mistakes,
or the bloodied newsprint
of despair.

Call me a fool once.
Call me a fool twice.
Call me a fool a hundred times.

I may spend many nights
nursing a broken heart—
but each time,
I will rise
to meet this world again.

With bright, unguarded eyes.
And I will seek wonder—
even when everything around me
smoulders.

44. Coming of Age

Love once had a softness to it—
like the timbre of morning prayer,
the tinkle of temple bells
enveloping me in joy and peace.

Love once came uninvited—
yet gently—
like sunlight slipping through
clouds on a misty winter morning,
warming my cold, cold feet.

When love touched me—
just a brush across my cheek—
coins leapt from wishing wells,
flinging themselves into the heavens.

At its peak, love was a beach house—
where I could sit by the window,
watch waves roll in,
walk barefoot in the sand,

fingers laced in magic.

But love is old now. Ailing.
It coughs blood.
It dresses in rags
and watches distant ships
with wistful eyes.

The wells are empty.
The mornings—smogged,
like vaporized poison.

And love?
It sputters.
Old, haggard, and inconvenient.
Wailing through the night—
wishing,
perhaps,
for an easy passing.

Part 7. A Universe Within – Awe and Re-enchantment

Even amidst brokenness, there remains a yearning for beauty, for wonder, for light. These poems speak to that flicker—a butterfly wing, a painted sky, a silent forest—that reminds us we are more than our grief. That love, in some forms, is eternal. That we belong to the stars.

45. I Will be There

Come—
find me in the soft flutter of butterfly wings,
lazing in the light of dawn's first sun.
See me drift along the bumbling brook,
hiding and seeking land,
swallowing flower petals in eddies between stones.

Feel me stretch across your eyes
on an autumn night—like a dream.
Taste the lilt of my hum
in the honeybees' labour.
Find me in the gentleness of floating clouds,
shapeshifting into your deepest desire.

I will sing for you on a rainy night—
the thunder my percussion.
I will wipe your tears
with every caress of my voice,
as you break down
to the ache of a lost lullaby.

I will linger
in the fragrance of the Earth
after monsoon rains have made love to it.
In the brush of wind against your skin,
you will feel my touch—

so that you'll know:
I am there.
Forevermore—
and even beyond.

46. Let's Paint the Sky Tonight

Let's paint the sky tonight.
Let's try an after-dinner fit—
of fantasy, not reruns.

Let's not lie and watch TV.
No—tonight,
let's paint the sky.

I'll take this corner of blue,
you take that patch of black.
Let's scatter stars across it all—
and meet somewhere in between,
on our shared canvas of night.

Let's bring down the box
we stored in the attic, long ago—
pull out old dreams,
and that bird-shaped cloud
you once showed me in spring.

Let's place them back in the sky,
for everyone to see.

And the glitter from '99,
when we first met—
why not dig it out from its grave?

Come on—
let's skip the rerun,
finish dinner early tonight.

Let's paint the sky starry—
you and I.

Part 8. The Land of Belonging

There comes a moment after the ache, after the fight, when the soul ceases to wrestle with time and begins to walk alongside it. This is the hush after the storm, where the self is no longer scattered across memories or longings but gathered—whole and holy. In these poems, time returns not as a thief but as a giver, and the speaker, having offered everything—patience, forbearance, pain— receives herself back in return. These are poems of return, of spiritual reckoning, of quiet arrival into one's own heart. This is the land of belonging.

47. Penance

Like a silver chime, I rattle in the winds,
moving gently to and from
the space that stretches
between longing and belonging.

Gently on some days,
and furiously on others—
the winds of time have their way.

Who can test the tempest of time?
The fiercest warriors
have been turned into sages,
and those who refused
dispatched to other worlds
or forced to bend the knee.

Kneeling at the altar of time,
here I am—
dignity neatly wrapped in robes of gold,
placed at time's feet,

with other gifts in tow.

What more can I offer today
to pacify time's fury?

Patience—my most precious virtue—
has long been in service of time.
Forbearance,
which I have gathered through years,
is also on offer today.

"Rise," the timbre echoes in my ears.
And I do as I'm told,
feeling the full weight of my years.

Dare I glance
at the scornful face of time today?
I do.
And what I see—was it a chuckle I imagined?

No fangs. Only a boyish grin.

Time takes my hand,
unwraps the presents I bore him,
steps forward,
kisses my forehead,
and whispers:

"These gifts are for you, dearest.
I offer them back to you."

Then, looking around, he declares:
"She has served me well.
And so, from today,
she no longer sways to and from.
I am sending her
to the Land of Belonging."

I would write more,
but my eyes are now misty—
for time's gifts are precious.
And he is forever
running out.

I won't pretend to chase him—
only spend my life
in gratitude.

48. Who Am I?

Am I the dream
that was dreamt on a midsummer's night—
the one that smelled
of a thousand lavender bouquets?

Or am I the slow burn
of a million cigarettes,
turning to ash
on the forgotten streets of September?

Am I the glow
of a thousand twilights,
breaking through the darkness
of lonely nights—
where lovers lie miles apart?

Or am I the silver sheen
that blankets the sky,
a full moon
draped in a thousand stars?

Who am I?

This question haunts me.
Sometimes, the mirror taunts me.

Am I the past
that slipped through my fingers?
The present
that aches upon my shoulders?
Or the future—
balancing somewhere between
hope and despair?

Who would know the answer to this?
I don't know.
I don't really know.

All I know
is that I am.

And like the sun that rises each day,
there is no denying
my existence.

Like the ebb and flow
of tides in the ocean,

answers come and go.

There are days of clarity,
and days of confusion.

Who am I?
Who really am I?

49. Grief - My Companion

Grief holds onto you—
filling the space between your fingers
with its tallow-like grip.

It slips, at times,
leaving you lighter—
if only for a moment.

And then,
it creeps up your throat,
squeezing your breath.

You hate your grief.
Others cower around it—
a pall that shrouds everything.

You wonder
why it won't leave you alone.

And then one day,

for no reason at all,
grief becomes your soulful companion—
holding your hand
through a journey
meant to be taken alone.

It plants roses in your trail.
And when you look back,
one day—
there is nothing
but a sea of flowers.

Your hands are waxy.
Your throat, a little scratchy.

But grief—
she has left you.

That suet on your fingers—
the only reminder
that she was once here.

50. Waiting to be Found

I've been losing myself lately—
in bits and pieces, in parts
that no longer feel like me.

I could tell you I'm lost,
but what words would suffice
to describe my condition?

A poet's rendition
is all I can muster—
and even that
feels less than what I feel.

No, words cannot describe
the scent of the fire
that rises from your hair,
or the saffron trail
I've been blindly following—
or the crowd
that left me behind.

In bits and pieces,
I tried to reinvent myself—
and now,
I'm no more familiar to me
than I am to you.

No,
I'm not a lost child anymore—
just a stranger
in a strange land,
hoping we might find me together,
after we find you.

51. Solar Flare

Today, I am a solar flare—
burning everything up.

The world turns slower than ever
as my work desk crumbles into ash
and rivers rise in steam
to meet the clouds.

I engulf everything—
the whirring of machines,
the smothering smog
that clings to tall buildings.

An intense burst of energy—
the unbearable lightness of being.

I am almost afraid
to close my eyes,
lest I find myself unrooted—
drifting through ether.

There's a faint calling.
I hear it from afar—
a call I've longed to answer,
time and time again.

Magnetic impulses pull me,
unbearably, toward you—
burning a clear path
through the blackened sky.

It's a call I can no longer ignore.

And as I beam through the dark,
rushing to melt into you,
I watch new stars form
from the cracks between us.

Something tugs at my heartstrings—
a harmony I almost forgot.

I am a solar flare today.
And I am flying home—
to finally become
a rainbow.

www.ingramcontent.com/pod-product-compliance
Lightning Source LLC
La Vergne TN
LVHW011029200726
843509LV00011B/1234